CW00649392

My Special Pony

RECORD BOOK

This book belongs to:

....

KENILWORTH PRESS
THE EQUESTRIAN PUBLISHER

Find your favourite photo of yourself and your special pony and stick it onto this page!

My Special
Pony
RECORD BOOK

Name ....

Age ....

Address ....

....

....

Tel number ....

School ....

Yard tel number ....

Vet ....

Farrier ....

Farrier's tel number ....

Stick a photo of your pony
here or write down more
details about your special
pony's distinguishing features.

My Special
Pony

Name ....
....

Stable name/nickname..................................
....

Date of birth..
....

Height..
....

Sex (gelding/mare/stallion)........................
....

Colour..
....

Passport No..
....

Breeding...
....

Sire...
....

Dam..
....

Date of arrival...
....

Bought from..
....

My Special Pony's
Colours and Markings

RIGHT OR OFFSIDE

Fill in the drawings with your pony's coat colour and mane, and any special features, like marks on the nose or on the legs. Are your pony's two sides identical?

LEFT OR NEAR SIDE

My Special Pony's ♡♡ Friends

How many four-legged friends does your special pony have? List their names and, if possible, stick in small photos of them.

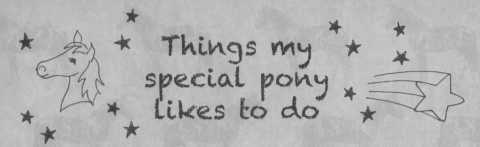

Things my special pony likes to do

Tick the boxes on a scale of 1 to 5

	1	2	3	4	5
Grazing					✓
Playing					✓
Snoozing					✓
Eating feeds					✓
Being groomed			✓		
Lying down					✓
Rolling in mud					6 ✓
Being nosey					✓

If you have a photo of your pony being naughty (as if!), stick it here

NAUGHTY THINGS MY SPECIAL PONY DOES!

How many things can you list here?

can you find an angelic photo of
your special pony to go here?

My Special Pony

	Yes	No
Good to catch?	✓	♡
Good to tack up?	✓	♡
Good to load?	✓	♡
Good to tie up?	✓	♡
Good to clip?	✓	♡
Good to groom?	✓	♡
Good to plait?	✓	♡
Good to lead?	✓	♡
Good to shoe?	✓	♡
Good in traffic?	✓	♡
Good in company?	✓	♡
Good to turn out?	✓	♡
Good in the stable?	✓	♡

Another photo opportunity for 'YOU KNOW WHO'. Use this space to stick in a photo of your special pony doing one of the activities opposite.

Activities

	Dislikes	Likes	Adores
Jumping			✓
Gymkhanas	✓		
Hacking out			✓
Hunting	✓		
Dressage	✓		
Pony clubbing		✓	
Picnic rides			✓
Showing			✓
Hunter trials	✓		
Eventing			✓

stick a photo of your
favourite horse or
rider here.

Hopes and Dreams

Which famous rider I'd like to
be for a day

....

Which famous competition horse
I'd most like to ride

....

What I'd like to achieve with
my SPECIAL pony

This month..

In a year's time...

In the future..

My greatest horsey ambition

....

Which major horse shows and events I've been to or would like to visit

Royal Windsor

Royal International

Horse of the Year Show

Olympia ✓

Badminton ✓

Bramham

Gatcombe

Burghley

Blenheim

Local county show ✓

(which one)

Others

Who I went with

What I learnt from the day

Photos or pictures in equine magazines
from the day

Take a photo of
your pony eating
his favourite treat,
and stick it onto
this page.

Things My Special
Pony Likes to Eat!

Make a list of your pony's favourite foods

My Pony Club

Branch name

District Commissioner's name

Pony club camp is held at

My favourite pony club rallies are (name them)

MY PONY CLUB FRIENDS

My special Pony club friends are

RIDERS

Name
..Holly..........

Name
..Eliza..........

Name
..Milly..........

Name
..Me..........

Name
..maisie..........

Name
..Lucy..........

PONIES

Pony's name
..na lulu..........

Pony's name
....

Pony's name
..Admird..........

Pony's name
..onchoa..........

Pony's name
..lady..........

Pony's name
..lolly..........

my PONY CIUb Badges

**Make a list of your Pony Club badges
(or if you are feeling artistic, why not draw them?)**

My Pony Club Tests

Make a list of the tests you have taken and the dates you passed them.

E test ....

D test ....

D+ test ....

C test ....

C+ test ....

B test ....

A test ....

Other tests ....

(Psssst... there's room to continue your list over here.)

My Pony Club Rally

Date ....

Place ....

Teacher ....

Type of Rally ....

....

How the Rally went ....

....

Which of my friends went ....

....

What I learned today ....

....

Any comments ....

....

My Pony Club
Rally

Date ....

Place ....

Teacher ....

Type of Rally ....

....

How the Rally went ....

....

Which of my friends went ....

....

What I learned today ....

....

Any comments ....

....

My Pony Club Rally

Date ....

Place ....

Teacher ....

Type of Rally ....

....

How the Rally went ....

....

Which of my friends went ....

....

What I learned today ....

....

Any comments ....

....

My Pony Club Rally

Date ....

Place ....

Teacher ....

Type of Rally ....
....

How the Rally went ....
....

Which of my friends went ....
....

What I learned today ....
....

Any comments ....
....

My Pony Club Rally

Date ....

Place ....

Teacher ....

Type of Rally ....

....

How the Rally went ....

....

Which of my friends went ....

....

What I learned today ....

....

Any comments ....

....

Dream shopping List

Write a list of the items you would like for yourself and your pony. Include details about sizes and colours — and just before Christmas or your birthday, leave this page open for others to see! (No harm in trying.)

For myself:

For my special pony:

Draw a map of a favourite ride here.
Show the places where you walk/trot/canter.

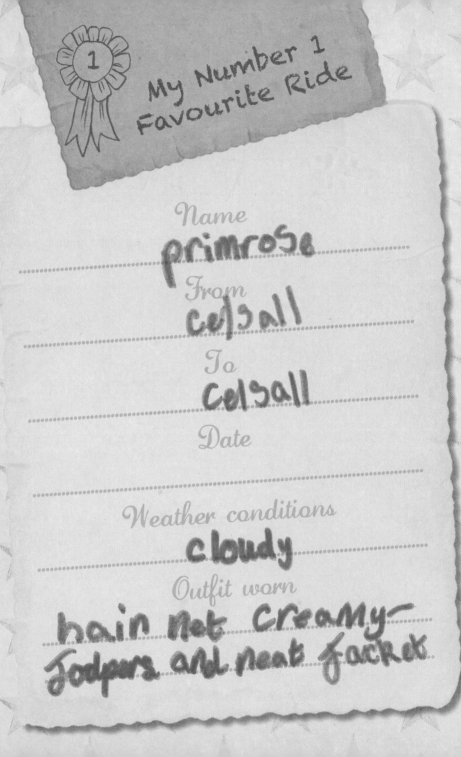

My Number 1 Favourite Ride

Name
primrose

From
celsall

To
celsall

Date

Weather conditions
cloudy

Outfit worn
hain net creamy-
Jodpers and neat Jacket

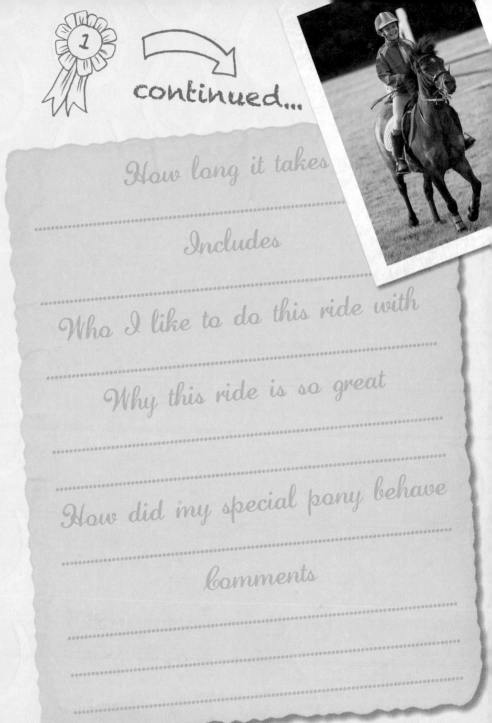

How long it takes

....

Includes

....

Who I like to do this ride with

....

Why this ride is so great

....

....

How did my special pony behave

....

Comments

....

....

....

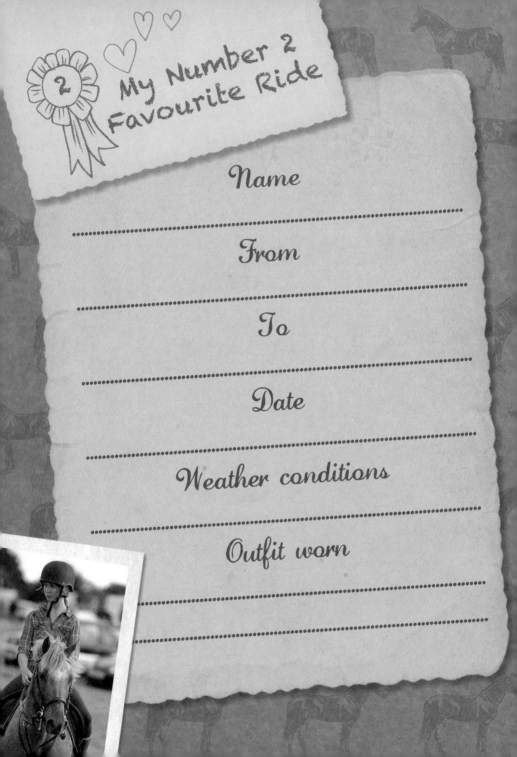

2 My Number 2
Favourite Ride

Name

....

From

....

To

....

Date

....

Weather conditions

....

Outfit worn

....

....

continued...

How long it takes

....

Includes

....

Who I like to do this ride with

....

Why this ride is so great

....

....

How did my special pony behave

....

Comments

....

....

....

My Number 3 Favourite Ride

Name

....

From

....

To

....

Date

....

Weather conditions

....

Outfit worn

....

....

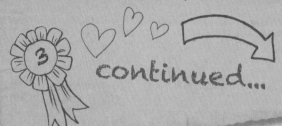

continued...

How long it takes

....

Includes

....

Who I like to do this ride with

....

Why this ride is so great

....

....

How did my special pony behave

....

Comments

....

....

....

Looking after *My Special* Pony

	THINGS I KNOW HOW TO DO (YES/NO)	THINGS I'D LIKE TO LEARN TO DO (YES/NO)
How to groom my special pony	✓	
How to put on a headcollar	✓	
How to put on a bridle	✓	
How to put on a saddle		✓
How to put on a stable rug	✓	
How to put on a New Zealand rug	✓	
How to plait a mane	✓	

	THINGS I KNOW HOW TO DO (YES/NO)	THINGS I'D LIKE TO LEARN TO DO (YES/NO)
How to plait a tail		✓
How to do quartermarks		✓
How to put on a tail bandage		✓
How to fill a haynet	✓	
How to wash down my pony	✓	✓
How to help clip my pony		✓
Know the points of the horse	✓	
Clean tack		✓
Oil hooves		✓
Other		✓

Pony Club Camp

Dates ....

Place ....

Teachers ....

List of lessons attended ....

....

....

My favourite day ....

What was the food like ....

....

How did my special pony behave

....

Which of my friends were there

....

What I learned most during the week

....

My special outfits ....

....

Marks for tack and turnout inspections ....
....

Marks for stable inspections ....
....

Any prizes/awards won by my special pony ....
....

Goals for next year ....
....

Pictures from camp

Pony Club Camp

Dates ....

Place ....

Teachers ....

List of lessons attended ....

....

....

My favourite day ....

What was the food like ....

....

How did my special pony behave

....

Which of my friends were there

....

What I learned most during the week

....

My special outfits ....

....

Marks for tack and turnout inspections ....

Marks for stable inspections ....

Any prizes/awards won by my special pony ....

Goals for next year ....

Pictures from camp

Pony Club Camp

Dates ....

Place ....

Teachers ....

List of lessons attended ....

....

....

My favourite day ....

What was the food like ....

....

How did my special pony behave

....

Which of my friends were there

....

What I learned most during the week

....

My special outfits ....

....

Marks for tack and turnout
inspections ....

....

Marks for stable inspections ....

....

Any prizes/awards won by my
special pony ....

....

Goals for next year ....

....

Pictures from camp

Pony Club Camp

Dates ....

Place ....

Teachers ....

List of lessons attended ....

....

....

My favourite day ....

What was the food like ....

....

How did my special pony behave

....

Which of my friends were there

....

What I learned most during the week

....

My special outfits ....

....

Marks for tack and turnout
inspections ....
....

Marks for stable inspections ....
....

Any prizes/awards won by my
special pony ....
....

Goals for next year ....
....

Pictures from camp

Stick a photo of you and
your special pony from
your first competition
here, or even your very
first rosette!

1

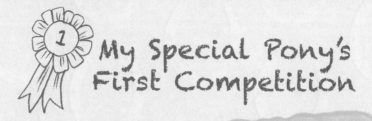

My Special Pony's First Competition

Date

Place

Type of competition

Class entered

Result

Prize

My special memory of that day

A photo of your
special pony all
togged up for the
show ring would
look good here.

My Special Pony's Competition Records

Date.......................... Place ....

Type of competition ....

....

Class(es) entered ....

....

Result(s) ....

Prize(s) ....

My special memory of that day

....

....

....

Tips for next time ....

....

....

More of
my special pony's
competition photos

More of my special pony's competition records

Date...................... Place ....

Type of competition ....

....

Class(es) entered ....

....

Result(s) ....

Prize(s) ....

My special memory of that day

....

....

....

Tips for next time ....

....

....

More of
my special pony's
competition photos

More of my special pony's competition records

Date...................... Place ....

Type of competition ....

....

Class(es) entered ....

....

Result(s) ....

Prize(s) ....

My special memory of that day

....

....

....

Tips for next time ....

....

....

More of
my special pony's
competition photos

More of my special pony's competition records

Date...................... Place ....

Type of competition ....
....

Class(es) entered ....
....

Result(s) ....

Prize(s) ....

My special memory of that day
....
....
....

Tips for next time ....
....
....

More of
my special pony's
competition photos

More of my special pony's competition records

Date........................ Place ....

Type of competition ....
....

Class(es) entered ....
....

Result(s) ....

Prize(s) ....

My special memory of that day
....
....
....

Tips for next time ....
....
....

More of
my special pony's
competition photos

Date........................ Place ....

Type of competition ....

....

Class(es) entered ....

....

Result(s) ....

Prize(s) ....

My special memory of that day

....

....

....

Tips for next time ....

....

....

More of my special pony's competition records

Date........................ Place ....

Type of competition ....

....

Class(es) entered ....

....

Result(s) ....

Prize(s) ....

My special memory of that day

....

....

....

Tips for next time ....

....

....

More of
my special pony's
competition photos

More of my special pony's competition records

Date........................ Place ....

Type of competition ....
....

Class(es) entered ....
....

Result(s) ....

Prize(s) ....

My special memory of that day
....
....
....

Tips for next time ....
....
....

More of my special pony's competition records

Date........................ Place ....

Type of competition ....
....

Class(es) entered ....
....

Result(s) ....

Prize(s) ....

My special memory of that day

....

....

....

Tips for next time ....

....

....

Date........................ Place ....

Type of competition ....
....

Class(es) entered ....
....

Result(s) ....

Prize(s) ....

My special memory of that day
....
....
....

Tips for next time ....
....
....

use this page to draw training exercises, make notes or to stick on photos of your pony in action

My Special
Pony

Lessons and Training Notes

Date ....

Place ....

Teacher ....

Type of lesson/training.......................................

....

How the lesson went..

What was learned ....

....

Things to remember for next time ....

....

....

use this page to draw training exercises, make notes or to stick on photos of your pony in action

more of My Special Pony

Lessons and Training notes

Date ....

Place ....

Teacher ....

Type of lesson/training.............................

....

How the lesson went................................

What was learned ....

....

Things to remember for next time ....

....

....

use this page to draw training exercises,
make notes or to stick on photos of your
pony in action

more of My Special
Pony

Lessons and Training notes

Date ....

Place ....

Teacher ....

Type of lesson/training...................................

....

How the lesson went...................................

What was learned ....

....

Things to remember for next time ....

....

....

use this page to draw training exercises, make notes or to stick on photos of your pony in action

more of My Special Pony

Lessons and Training Notes

Date ....

Place ....

Teacher ....

Type of lesson/training...

....

How the lesson went..

What was learned ....

....

Things to remember for next time ....

....

....

use this page to draw training exercises, make notes or to stick on photos of your pony in action

more of My Special Pony

Lessons and Training Notes

Date ....

Place ....

Teacher ....

Type of lesson/training.......................................

....

How the lesson went..

What was learned ....

....

Things to remember for next time ....

....

....

more of My Special Pony

Lessons and Training Notes

Date ....

Place ....

Teacher ....

Type of lesson/training...

....

How the lesson went...

What was learned ....

....

Things to remember for next time ....

....

....

use this page to draw training exercises, make notes or to stick on photos of your pony in action

more of My Special Pony

Lessons and Training notes

Date ....

Place ....

Teacher ....

Type of lesson/training..

....

How the lesson went..

What was learned ....

....

Things to remember for next time ....

....

....

use this page to draw training exercises,
make notes or to stick on photos of your
pony in action

more of My Special Pony

Lessons and Training notes

Date ....

Place ....

Teacher ....

Type of lesson/training ....
....

How the lesson went ....

What was learned ....
....

Things to remember for next time ....
....
....

Stable
management

on-
chon

Farriery dates	:	Type of visit	:	name of vet

Stable
management

Farriery dates	Type of visit	Name of vet

My Favourite
Special Pony Jokes

For notes and doodles

For notes and doodles

For notes and doodles

For notes and doodles

Copyright © 2013 Kenilworth Press

First published in the UK in 2008
by Kenilworth Press, an imprint of Quiller Publishing Ltd
This updated edition published in 2013

British Library Cataloguing-in-Publication Data
A catalogue record for this book
is available from the British Library

ISBN 978 1 905693 94 8

All rights reserved. No part of this book may be reproduced
or transmitted in any form or by any means, electronic or
mechanical including photocopying, recording or by any
information storage and retrieval system, without permission
from the Publisher in writing.

Illustrations by Sally Bostock Leggatt and Kath Grimshaw
Designed by Kath Grimshaw
Photographs by Julian Preston (cover, p25, 35, 36, 38)
Megan Price (p11), West Hollowcombe Farm (p89)
Printed in China

KENILWORTH PRESS
THE EQUESTRIAN PUBLISHER

Kenilworth Press
An imprint of Quiller Publishing Ltd
Wykey House, Wykey, Shrewsbury, SY4 1JA
Tel: 01939 261616 Fax: 01939 261606
E-mail: info@quillerbooks.com
Website: www.kenilworthpress.co.uk

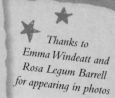

*Thanks to
Emma Windeatt and
Rosa Legum Barrell
for appearing in photos*